# The Giant Who Drank from His Shoe

## and other stories

# The Giant Who Drank from His Shoe

## and other stories

**Léonce Bourliaguet**

**Illustrated by Gerald Rose**

Translated by John Buchanan-Brown

**A Grasshopper Book**
**Abelard-Schuman**
**London**

Selected from *Le Marchand de Nuages*

First published in England 1966
This edition 1974



ISBN 0 200 72109 7 (hardback)
ISBN 0 200 72085 6 (paperback)

Abelard-Schuman Limited
450 Edgware Road
London W2

24 Market Square
Aylesbury, Buckinghamshire

Printed in Great Britain

# Contents

# *The Giant Who Drank from His Shoe*

Long ago, in the Thirteenth Century, there lived a giant who used to wander across France, strolling from province to province. As he went, his usual round would take him from Périgord to Limousin, and when you were at Pierre-Buffière and saw him coming, it was like a storm gathering on the horizon. For he was so huge that he had to bend his head a little to stop bumping it on the clouds.

And when they saw this mass darkening the heavens, the people would cry in their alarm: "Woe! Woe! Our two plagues are upon us again!"

The first plague was that their harvest was flattened wherever the giant set his great feet. But that was nothing compared to the rest, and the rest was this. The giant had come a long way, and his walk made him very thirsty indeed. So he would sit down, take off his shoe, fill it with water from a handy river or

lake, lift it high, high up to his lips and then he would drink. Glu . . . glu . . . glug. After that he would shake his shoe dry over the surrounding countryside before putting it back on his foot.

Now, in the toe of his shoe, apart from the drop of water which had not gone down his throat, there would lurk the rocks and boulders which he had scooped up from the bed of the lake or river. Thus it was that five or six parishes suffered not only from a slight rain storm, but from a positive hail of huge boulders which came whistling down like bombs and plunged into the ground all over the place, in the woods, in the meadows and among the standing corn.

The poor people of Limousin cowered for safety under this barrage of boulders in the nearest convenient hole in the ground and did not dare come out again until the giant had departed. However, they discovered that this did not happen to the people in nearby Périgord.

"Doesn't the giant really shower boulders upon your heads?" one of them asked, having gone to Périgord especially to find out.

"Wherever would he get the boulders from?" was the answer. "There aren't any in our wine vats!"

"In your vats?"

"Of course, in our vats. You see we fill the giant's shoe with wine."

The man returned, bubbling over with the news and told the whole Viscounty of Limoges that, when you offered the giant wine, he did not scrape the lakes and rivers for a drink of water. The people of Limousin resolved to copy this idea, but, alas, in those days their country was too cold for vines to grow. If they were to offer the giant a shoeful of wine they would have to buy it from the people of Périgord. This they did; and the people of Périgord sold them the very worst casks they had.

When the inhabitants of Pierre-Buffière saw the giant looming on the horizon, like a storm cloud, they hurried off to meet him with twenty carts laden with barrels. The giant took off his shoe and filled it with the dregs which the people of Périgord had sold them.

However, before he drank it he sniffed it and then he exclaimed in a voice like thunder: "My little men, you've given me vinegar instead of wine!"

The poor folk thought that in his disappointment the giant would squash them flat as pancakes under his huge feet. But nothing happened, and at last after standing there, holding his shoe with a pleased but hesitant expression on his face, the giant spoke.

"I feel like a good green salad. I've got the vinegar, but what about the oil?"

The people of Limousin still shivered in their shoes as they answered that they had oil, too.

"What's it made of?"

"Poppy seed, your Highness!"

"Pooh! The only oil I like is walnut oil!"

Then a crafty man in the crowd piped up: "They have as much as you want in Périgord!"

"Then I'd better go back," said the giant.

So he turned on his heel and headed south, stepping very gingerly so as not to spill his shoe full of good vinegar.

The people of Périgord were dumbfounded when they saw the giant loom over their province once more. Down he sat, set his hat (it was as round as a salad-bowl) between his knees, took off his other shoe and demanded walnut oil in a voice like thunder.

They had to drain the oil presses of the four baronies of Périgord to fill the other shoe.

The next thing the giant said was: "And now for the garlic!"

It needed three carts full to provide enough garlic, and they had to borrow some from the people of Quercy.

When they had brought the cartloads of garlic, peeled it and thrown it into the vast salad bowl of a hat, there was a fresh rumble of thunder from the giant.

"Salt and pepper!"

They had to go as far afield as Saintonge for the salt, and Toulouse for the pepper. And even that wouldn't have been enough if they hadn't mixed in five thousand pounds of best lime from Saint-Astier when the giant wasn't looking.

"Good!" said the giant. "Good! We've got the dressing, now, what about the green stuff? What I'd like are dandelions!"

Dandelions! Heavens above! Dandelion leaves hidden in the long grass! They needed thirty carts full; so young and old, man and woman, every single

person in Périgord had to go out to collect dandelions. Even the children were given a holiday from school to help. And when they had finished you would have thought you were in a land of hunchbacks, so hard it was for the poor people to straighten up again.

But at last the giant had everything he had asked for and he could eat his salad.

When he had swallowed the last morsel, he smacked his lips contentedly and said: "What a grand little place this is! It's got everything I want. If that's the way it is, then this is where I'll stay for the rest of my days."

And he was as true as his word. And so for the next thirty years the people of Périgord were forced to serve him with food and drink by the cartload. In the end he died and the Devil carried him off, but the Province was ruined!

And from that day to this, to fill their purses once more, the people of Périgord have been forced to sell their best wine to the people of Limousin and to drink their worst wine themselves.

# *Clouds for Sale*

One day, when Saint Peter was balancing his accounts, he found that there was a shortage. It was nothing very much, a matter of fifteen broad pieces as gold as the sun, and three pieces as silver as the moon. But small as the amount was, his accounts were short and he would have to make them good as quickly as he could.

And the sooner he did so the better, for, if God the Father were to notice, he would certainly suspect that all was not well with the Great Ledger Book of Heaven. Then the Infallible Auditor would look into it and his examination of the debits and credits might well reveal other, much bigger mistakes.

So Saint Peter determined to do something at once. He disguised himself as a pedlar of almanacs and, with his angelic aide-de-camp at his heels, came swooping down to Earth. There, he wandered from town to town in search of a loan from rich men, from bankers, from misers, from all who hatch fat bags of broad gold pieces. But not one of them would lend him so much as a farthing. The Saint was bitterly disappointed.

"Let's throw these wretched almanacs away," he said to his angelic aide-de-camp, "get rid of our disguises, and fly back to Heaven!"

And there they were in all their glory, Saint Peter and the young angel, about to take wing, when up came an old clothes man.

The rogue knew who they were at once.

He took off his hat, flung himself down on his knees, his arms going like windmills as he crossed himself over and over again, babbled an "Our Father" or two, and then, when these formalities were over, he rose to his feet and said: "Oh, Mighty Saint! Great Saint Peter! Haven't you anything to sell me?"

"I'm afraid I haven't, my son."

"Come, come! What about your angel's worn out breeches?"

"My angels don't wear breeches, my son."

"Well then, Mighty Saint, what about those rags up there?"

"What rags up there?"

"The ones floating above our heads, Mighty Saint!"

And the old clothes man pointed to some tattered clouds gently puffed by the breeze across the blue sky.

"Clouds? Do you really want to buy some clouds from me?"

"Indeed I do! I've wanted to deal in clouds for some time now. It's a little idea of my very own."

"Well I never," Saint Peter murmured after a few moments' thought. "Well I never! There's nothing to stop me from letting the fellow have what he wants. There are plenty of clouds, and no one will notice the difference if I sell him one or two . . . and anyway, it won't be for long! Now, my son, I'm prepared to make a deal with you. For fifteen broad pieces as gold as the sun, and for three pieces as silver as the moon, you may have all the clouds which float over your head. And I'll do more for you than that, I'll let you have something which will enable you to make the clouds go wherever you want them. Gabriel, be a good angel and go back to heaven and find my little white flute. Hurry now!"

In less than five minutes, the angelic aide-de-camp had done what he had been told.

"But I can't play the flute," the old clothes man grumbled. "You haven't a hurdy-gurdy, have you?"

"Don't you worry," the saint replied. "All you have to do is blow into the flute, and the clouds will follow you wherever you want them to go. Now listen carefully to what I say. When you have earned ten times the amount you are going to give me, you must return the flute to me . . . and no nonsense, mind you!"

The old clothes man agreed to these terms, paid the fifteen gold pieces and the three silver ones and they parted the best of friends.

When the saint and the angel had gone, the old clothes man tried out his powers. He blew, and out of the three holes in the little white flute came a tune which served as a signal to the clouds floating above his head. They formed in a line behind him and followed him as passively as a herd of cows coming home for milking.

Then the old clothes man, who knew very well what he was doing, set off for those parts of the country which suffer most from drought.

When he came to some province frizzling in the sun, he would stop his fluting to cry: "Clouds! Who wants a cloud? Rain at your doorstep! Who wants a cloud?"

And, of course everyone came to buy.

As he took their money, the rogue would cry: "Here! You long streak of rainwater, Stratus! Go with the gentleman and water his cornfield!"

Or else it would be: "Here! You great fat Cumulus! Go with the lady and water her garden!"

And the clouds did exactly what they were told. Of course there were the unruly ones which tried to run away, but the buyer had only to set his dog on them and wave a stick at them, for the clumsy creatures to come back and get on with their job of watering the land.

And so it was that our hero had earned, not ten times, but a hundred times his loan to Saint Peter, before the saint remembered the peculiar transaction.

God the Father said to him one day: "It's a funny thing, but nowadays I don't seem to be getting any prayers from the places which suffer most from drought. It's a long time since I had a procession. Do you think mankind has found a way of making artificial rain? Peter! You'll have to go down and see what is going on!"

"Goodness gracious!" thought Saint Peter. "I'd

forgotten all about it! It's high time I got my little white flute back from that old clothes man. It's as plain as plain that he's the cause of what the Good Lord has noticed."

Instantly he returned to Earth, appeared in front of the old clothes man and asked him for the return of his flute.

"Oh! Mighty Saint!" exclaimed the man with clouds for sale. "I've only earned nine times what I gave you. Please let me keep the flute just a little longer. The Count of Toulouse has asked me to go to Languedoc."

And nothing Saint Peter could say made any difference.

So the mighty saint, who did not wish to lower himself to undignified haggling, simply said to the old clothes man: "My son, you will be very sorry that you did not keep your side of the bargain."

With this he walked away and, before flying up to Heaven, signalled to a passing bee to come close to his lips. The saint whispered something to the bee and the bee carried out its orders to the letter. It seized its chance while the wicked old clothes man was having a drink on the terrace of a wayside inn, and blocked one of the three holes in the little white flute with a piece of wax so cleverly placed that the man never noticed the difference.

He was, in any case, in a great hurry to reach Languedoc, whither he really had been summoned. The Count of Toulouse feared that a drought was beginning, which would ruin the harvest, a particularly fine one, as it happened, that year.

Between Garidech and Montpitol, the old clothes man slackened speed and began to blow on his flute to collect the clouds behind him, for he wished to enter Toulouse at the head of an imposing cavalcade.

But, merciful Heaven, goats, not clouds, collected to the new tune from the flute! And not the goats of Garidech and Montpitol alone! There were goats

from Giroussens and Bondigoux, and Monbéqui and Pessoulens and Tourrenquets. And these were only the vanguard. Behind them streamed all the goats of the Causses, Rouergue and Ségala, while the rear was swelled by the goats from Larzac, from the hills around Lacaune and from the Black Mountain!

Meanwhile the old clothes man strutted on his way to Toulouse, too stupid to realize that the flute was only playing on two holes now, and firmly believing that an army of clouds was at his heels, not an army of goats ten thousand strong. There were old goats, young goats, billy-goats and nanny-goats, not one of them uttering so much as a bleat. They did not utter so much as a bleat because their mouths were full, and their mouths were full because they devoured everything in their path, young corn, old cabbages, lettuces, everything right down to the

garlic. And you can imagine what a disaster that was to the inhabitants! I suppose it was one answer to the drought, for after that herd had passed there was not a plant left for the sun to scorch.

Our hero realized something was wrong only when the people recovered from their shock and began to shout at him. In his terror he dropped down on all fours among the goats and crept away in the confusion. And so although they had the gallows ready for him, they never caught him. In his flight he dropped the little white flute, and the poor little angel sent for that purpose had a hard task finding it. But there it was in a bundle of asparagus in the market at Toulouse, where, in her innocence, short-sighted old Mother Catherine had stuck it.

# *The Eagles' Promise*

It was so cold that winter that not a creature could live on the mountain. The frost split the rocks and the trees. The valleys re-echoed the thunder of the avalanches and when the noise died away you could almost feel the silence, so deathly quiet it was. What is more it was hard to tell night from day, but for the twinkling stars in the clear sky, such a mysterious radiance was cast by the pure white snow.

And so all the creatures of the high peaks, the lynx, the buzzard, the capercailzie, the wild cat, the bear and the marmot were driven down to the lowlands to survive.

In their train an eaglet sought refuge with the kindly hens in the valley. Now this all happened before Man had tamed these excellent fowl. They lived in freedom and roosted at night in the branches of the trees. When winter came they would shelter in the caves, warm in the depths of the earth. There in the opening of this natural poultry house, stood the eaglet and asked to be allowed in.

"Dear hens, in the sacred name of hospitality, please take me in," he begged them.

The oldest chicken thought there was something nice about this odd looking stranger—she had never seen an eagle close to, let alone an eaglet in all the pride of his youth—and so she replied: "Handsome stranger, we will take you in for as long as this cruel winter lasts, if you will swear on this tuft of feathers, that you will never harm us."

The eaglet took the oath of perpetual peace on a tuft of feathers. He promised by heart, liver and gizzard, and really meant what he said. And so he was taken into the comfort of the underground poultry house and passed the winter peacefully with his kind sisters, the hens.

At the same time another eaglet, a female this time, sought refuge with the kindly rabbits of the valley.

There she stood at the entrance of their vast warren and asked to be allowed in. "Dear rabbits, in the sacred name of hospitality, please take me in," she begged them.

The oldest rabbit thought that there was something nice about this odd-looking stranger—he had never

seen an eagle close to, let alone an eaglet in the full bloom of her youth—and so he replied: "Fair stranger, we will take you in for as long as this cruel winter lasts, if you will swear on this tuft of fur that you will never harm us."

The eaglet took this oath of perpetual peace on a tuft of fur. She promised by heart, liver and gizzard, and really meant what she said. And so she was taken into the comfort of the warren and passed the winter peacefully among her kind brothers, the rabbits.

When Spring returned and the sun shone like a great golden dahlia in the blue sky, up into the air swept the eaglet. (From now on we shall call him "the tercel" because this is the proper name of all male eagles and other hawks.) The kind hens were frightened out of their wits by the spread of his wings, but as he swept in vast circles above their heads, the tercel, who was now full-grown, called down to them: "Dear hens, I shall never forget your kindness, and I shall always be your friend as I have promised!"

And from then on he really was the friend of the hens. He would often return to circle above their scarlet combs, with a kindly word for them when he had heard their news.

Meanwhile he hunted rabbits and only rabbits.

In her turn the eaglet emerged from the warren belonging to the kind rabbits and swept up into the air. Her hosts were scared out of their wits by the spread of her wings, but as she swooped in vast circles above their long ears, the eagle, who was now full-grown, called down to them: "Dear rabbits, I shall never forget your kindness, and I shall always be your friend as I have promised!"

And from then on she really was the friend of the rabbits. She would often return to circle above their long ears, with a kindly word for them when she had heard their news.

Meanwhile she hunted hens and only hens.

Now the eagle was very beautiful, as the tercels of the mountain soon discovered. They all began to court her and, to win her approval, each would hunt for her, bringing what they would call "a tasty bit of game"—in other words a plump and juicy little hen.

Of course, the eagle was bound by her promise not to harm rabbits, and thus grew so dreadfully tired of chicken that she decided to go on a hunger-strike. Angrily she refused the same eternally boring diet of fowl, rebuffed her uncomprehending suitors and went sadly away to her fast in the fastness of the highest peaks.

And so, when our tercel joined the ranks of her admirers and, unable by his oath to offer her the same tasty morsel as the others, brought her a rabbit, how she recovered her appetite! She accepted him at once. They set up house together and for one whole week the happy groom had to bring his bride rabbit after rabbit, so greedy had she become for their taste.

When the week was up, the eagle noticed that her

tercel was only pecking half-heartedly at his food.

"Whatever is the matter, my dear? Have you a chill or something?"

"Oh, darling it's this rabbit day after day."

"Don't let that upset you. Let me take my turn in fetching our food."

And the eagle swooped down into the valley upon a hen, which the tercel ate with the greatest of pleasure, as indeed did she—she was growing rather tired of rabbit.

And from that day forward, the eagle would find one sort of food for the larder and the tercel the other. Rabbit and chicken, chicken and rabbit, it was perfect.

"The drumstick, dear?"

"A little more leg of rabbit, my darling?"

Never did a young couple dine so delightfully.

The hens could not complain, nor could the rabbits; the eagles had kept their word.

And because their diet was varied, the eagle and the tercel were given health of body.

What is more, because neither had broken the promise made on a tuft of feathers and a tuft of fur, they were both granted peace of mind as well.

# *The Three Bears and the Baker*

That winter, when the three bears went to hibernate, neither the Father nor the Mother Bear nor their little cub could go to sleep. Simple and honest animals that they were, feeding on roots and shoots and wild honey, it could hardly have been black coffee that kept them awake. It must have been through eating too many myrtles, or perhaps too many rhododendron seeds.

Be it as it may, if you cannot sleep, you need to eat. Now the mountainside was deep with snow and the Father Bear found it very hard to give his mate and his cub anything but the sound advice to lick their paws in patience.

This only succeeded for a time, and then the Mother Bear said to her faithful husband: "Why don't you go to the men in the village at the foot of the mountain? But do be careful. You mustn't frighten them. If you dance on your hind legs you might make them laugh. And if you whined through your nose like a dog you might make them feel sorry for you and give you a truss of onions, or a cabbage or two, or else a few potatoes!"

"Humph!" said the Father Bear. "It's as plain as a pikestaff that if nobody helps us we'll starve to death. And if you're going to die, one way's as good as another, so I'm ready to risk going down to the village. But the first time I do it, I'll go after dark, to find out the lie of the land and get used to the scent of men."

The very next night the bear came down from the mountain, beneath which the village slumbered, deep in snow. The stars glittered frostily in the dark sky above as the lumbering old Father Bear was first attracted by the smell of smoke. On he went, for there is no smoke without a fire, and where there is a fire there is warmth. Soon he sniffed fresh bread, and there at the end of a narrow alley was the red glow of the village bakery.

You see, while everyone else was fast asleep, the baker was up and about, preparing his bread for the next day.

Then the bear stood in the open doorway, dancing on his hind legs and whining through his nose just as his wife had told him.

The baker turned around sharply.
He saw the bear.
His blood ran cold.
He waited to be gobbled up.

Then he realized that the animal was there to beg freshly-baked bread and not to attack him at all.

Once he was sure of this, the baker regained his confidence and took matters firmly in hand, exclaiming: "Aha, old chap? What are you hanging round here for? Come to give me a hand, have you? You've got the right ideas! Here, pass me those faggots and I'll give you some bread as a reward."

The bear did as he was told. He passed the faggots, put the bread in the oven, cleaned out the bakehouse and took the bread out of the oven when it was done. After working all night as hard as the best baker's boy, he was given a loaf of bread for his wages. He took it back to his cave, and that day the Bear family feasted on freshly-baked bread.

After this, every night the bear would go down to the bakery to help the baker, for he made the bread for all the villages on that particular side of the mountain. The man grew fond of his silent, hard-working assistant, satisfied with a loaf of bread for his wages. And then, as you might guess, the baker was not a little pleased with himself for having tamed a bear. Not everyone has a bear as a workmate, not even in the mountains.

One night the baker's wife got up especially to

watch this extraordinary hand at work.

"If only he were married," she said to her husband. "Then his wife could come and give me a hand in the house!"

The honest old thing heard what she said and told his mate about it. So the Mother Bear followed him down to the bakery and went into service with the baker's wife. Both bears worked so well and cost so little that within a few weeks the baker and his wife decided that they must live in. So the bears were given a stable with plenty of straw and made one last trip to their old cave to bring down their cub, and when winter was over and the mountainside was fresh and green, there were the three bears quite at home in the village among folk who, once their first burst of curiosity had been satisfied, took not a scrap of notice of them.

On their side, the bears, now that they had good bread in their bellies, quite forgot that they were bears, if in fact they had ever known that that is what they were.

Now it happened that the baker and his wife had a little boy who went to school in the tiny cottage at the other end of the village. The boy grew so fond of the bear cub that he would not be parted from him, so "little Bruin" was sent to join the other pupils. The schoolteacher was delighted to have him. She

could see nothing but good coming from having in the classroom a big, strong bear cub who was as good as gold and as quiet as a mouse. And best of all, if ever the School Inspector came around, he would not stay for long and would surely never come back again.

All the same, when "little Bruin" had grown so big that no desk could hold him without collapsing under his weight, the schoolteacher grew more concerned for her furniture. She therefore advised the baker and the Father and Mother Bear to apprentice him to some trade. When not one of them could make up their mind which to chose, they drew lots from little pieces of paper on which the schoolteacher had written; *Tailor*, *Painter*, *Chimney Sweep*, *Woodcutter* . . . and *Butcher*, the one they drew. Father Bear and the baker went down to the market town in the valley and placed "little Bruin" at once. He cried when he said good-bye to his father and to the kind baker, and even Father Bear's honest, beary eyes were misty. But they pulled themselves together, for they would not be long apart.

The two fathers walked back to their village high on the side of the mountain. The baker was well content to be rid of the member of the bear family who did no work. The Father Bear seemed to have his head in the clouds and was so lost in thought that the Mother Bear noticed something. "What's the matter, husband? You do look odd!"

"I don't quite know what a butcher is," the Father Bear replied. "But I'll tell you something: there's a lovely smell about a butcher's shop, and it carries right out into the street. Our cub's going to be all right."

Now, I should add at this point that matters had been so swiftly concluded with the butcher outside the shop, that the Father Bear had not so much as set foot inside.

But he could not forget the smell and so, a week later when the cub was allowed home to see his parents, he questioned him to find out more about it.

"My boy, what do you have to do for the butcher? What sort of job is it? . . . What exactly do you *butch*?"

"Well, Father, I help the butcher kill the sheep that the men eat."

"Eh? Do men eat wool, then?"

"Father, under the wool there's skin."

"So men eat skin."

"Under the skin there are bones, Father."

"Then men eat bones?"

"Under the wool, Father, and between the bones

and the skin, there's meat! That's what men eat!"

"Good gracious!" said Father Bear. "I'm not ashamed to say I never knew that, those crafty old sheep keep very dark about their . . . what did you call it . . . ah . . . their *meat*. I didn't know what it was, and I'd never even heard the word. But there's a very interesting and exciting smell about you. The next time you come home, my boy, bring your mother and me a piece of this *meat* stuff. We'd like to know just what it is."

You can guess what happened. The next time he was allowed home, the bear cub brought his parents a couple of juicy mutton chops which he had stolen from his master. No sooner had the Mother and the Father Bear tasted meat than their bread seemed so dull that it was no longer worth working so hard to earn it. Suddenly they turned savage, gobbled up the baker, the baker's wife and the baker's boy and fled to their old home in the cave, taking their cub with them.

It is since this Great Discovery that they like to vary their menu of fruit and wild honey with the occasional leg of mutton.

How silly that schoolteacher was, to have written *Butcher* on one of those pieces of paper! Had it been me, I should have written *Chemist*, *Cobbler*, or *Lamplighter*, and none of this would have happened and bears would still be happily vegetarian!

# *The Old Woman and the Birds*

Once upon a time there was a poor little old humpbacked woman who went out every day alone, with only her shadow for company, over the fields to gather dandelion leaves for her salad. In the evening she went home to her cottage on the edge of the forest. It was a humble dwelling of bits and pieces, thatched with old straw, and looking so wretched that a rat would have been ashamed to have been seen inside it.

Now so long as she only gathered dandelion leaves, the birds took no notice of her. But, one fine day, the Jay, who sees everything that goes on, made a surprising discovery. "The old woman" as they used to call her, had found a new task for herself.

She no longer gathered dandelion leaves!

She gathered wool!

The wool that belonged to the birds!

This is the wool that the sheep leave on the thorns and brambles in the hedgerows. There are little tufts of it everywhere, and when the time comes for them to build their nests, the birds collect it. What a fluttering and a twittering there is, as each little bird takes a strand in the tip of its beak! The wool makes a warm lining for the nest, which will soon be a home for its babies. How lovely it is in the warm spring sunshine when it is time to build a nest!

Until then the birds had had no rival in their delightful task. But now, here was this old woman

busily stealing the wool almost from under their little nestlings. Now this was something which must not be allowed to go on! Certainly not!

The first thing to be done was to call a meeting, to which the Jay, proud of the task given to him, summoned everyone.

And so, there in a clearing in the forest, birds of all shapes and sizes assembled in a Parliament of Fowls.

Once more the Jay told the story of what he had

seen, and there were a hundred witnesses to back the tale.

"That old thief," he said, "you'd never believe the amount of wool—of our wool I should say—she's picked off the hedgerows. Her hovel must be full of it. No doubt she plans, the old wretch, to turn it into a mattress thicker than the one the king's own daughter sleeps on."

The Robin, whose chest is a proud Republican red, hated the Jay whose feathers are splashed with Royalist blue. So he immediately rose to contradict him.

"A mattress! Wherever did our friend the Jay discover this tale of a mattress? His imagination is a little too vivid! We can't really condemn this old woman on the gossip of a Jay! In all fairness we should send someone sensible to find out the facts of the case."

The Parliament of Fowls passed his motion. The Wren was chosen to find out what was going on in the hovel, because he was so small that he could enter any nook and cranny.

Hard as he worked, it took the Wren many a visit to carry out properly the task entrusted to him. In fact it took him the whole summer, and many were the reports which he made to the other birds.

First he had to tell them that "the old woman" had not collected nearly so much wool as they had

thought. The poor old thing had only enough to fill her distaff once.

"And now, her crabbed old fingers set her wheel whirling and she spins, friends, how she spins!"

The second thing he had to tell them was that the spinning was over and that the wool was now rolled into a great fat ball.

"And now her crabbed old fingers hold a pair of needles and she knits, friends, she knits as though she'd never stop!"

The third thing the Wren had to tell the other birds was that this wool had been used to knit a pair of thick stockings.

"And now her old crabbed fingers have packed them into a parcel, friends, and the parcel has gone to Perlimpopolis!"

The birds were inquisitive to learn to whom these stockings had been sent. "It may even be to the king," they twittered. And so they sent the Heron of the Marshes to find out. They sent the Heron because it was winter now, a bitter winter, and he alone could fly through the cold white snow and the biting grey winds.

And so the Heron of the Marshes made his way to Perlimpopolis on this mission. He returned bursting with important news.

"Friends," he told the assembled birds, "do you know, the old woman has two sons? They are twins, and so much alike that you can hardly tell them apart. They are so tall, so strong and so handsome, that the king will have none but them to mount guard at the door of his palace. I saw them one snowy morning and I could not help admiring them, because there they were, standing one on either side of the door, holding their halberds and looking extremely elegant."

An old Magpie thought that there was more than met the eye in this "looking extremely elegant", and asked the Heron what he meant. Then the Heron had to admit that the old woman's two sons stood on guard in the snow like the wading birds, each with one foot on the cold ground and the other curled up under him.

"Just listen to that stupid great bird!" the Magpie exclaimed. "Can't you see that the poor woman could only send her sons one pair of stockings? And the boys, like the good brothers that they are, shared the pair between them, so that each can only keep one foot warm—the one they stand on? Friends, the other one is bare, and that is why the poor things curl it up under them!"

It was as plain as the nose on your face.

The kind hearts of the birds were so touched, that all, without exception, resolved to bring the old lady enough wool to knit another pair of stockings. They set to work at once. The old woman looked up, and there was a cloud of chaffinches and goldfinches, greenfinches and sparrows. By the time the morning was over they had refilled her distaff, and the old woman began to spin and to knit with such a will that, before the snow melted, her sons had stockings for their curled-up feet and could put them on the ground again. The Heron was the only one to feel sorry.

"Pooh!" he said. "Now they stand on their two feet like everybody else."

# *Palkin*

Away in the heart of Russia there lived a little boy. Every day he would take his father's cow to a clearing in the forest, as it was his task to guard the animals until he was old enough to go to school.

Truth to tell, he was in no hurry to start his schooling, for the school master was renowned as a boxer of ears.

Not that Mikolai—for that was the name of the little boy—had a more tender-hearted father. He strictly forbade his son to play games of any description while he was looking after the herd.

"You mustn't take your eyes off them for an instant," he told him. "If one of my animals loses a horn or a tail, or strangles or chokes or catches a cold, why, I'll skin you alive!"

It was too much to expect the lad to sit alone all day long in the forest watching the cows chewing the cud. And so, secretly, while not always keeping so keen an eye upon his charges, he would take his knife and carve faces on the sticks he stripped from the bushes.

He best liked slips of box, that hard, honey-toned aristocrat of woods.

He soon became so skilled that the faces of men and women which his knife created looked as though they were alive. And yet he was never content with his work and would throw it into a little stream which removed the evidence of his neglectful cow keeping.

His first masterpiece was a distaff. On the tall point he carved the face of a lovely girl. Her features were so lofty and noble and her expression so melting and so deep that Mikolai's heart began to flutter. He hid his work in a holly thicket, because he wanted to be the only person in the world to know of Kunkel—for that was the name he had given to the lifelike little figurehead—whom he would not have dreamed of taking back to his father's farm.

His second masterpiece was a walking stick. On its head, he carved the face of a handsome young man whom he called Palkin. Palkin had all the gravity and charm of Kunkel and, where her eyes were tender, his in addition had a glint of courage and of energy. Mikolai was so pleased with it that he stuck the stick in a tall clump of gorse. He wanted to be the only friend in the world of this lifelike little figurehead, whom he would not have dreamed of taking back to his father's farm.

And afterwards all the skill in his knife was spent on

carving animals' heads—cats, dogs, lizards and frogs—but the long hours of his watching were lightened by the presence of Kunkel and Palkin in their prickly prisons. He would spend an hour first with one and then with the other, but the idea of bringing them together never crossed his mind. Oh, no: he kept them strictly apart, neither knowing of the other's existence.

However, one day, Mikolai noticed that Palkin must have sensed or guessed that Kunkel was there, for the handsome walking stick with the carved head had jumped out of the gorse bush and hopped unhindered on its tip to where the beautiful distaff stood in the clump of holly. He caught them together, each smiling, it was so happy to be with the other.

In his rage, Mikolai set the blade of his knife to Palkin's face once more, marring it with wens and warts and wrinkles. When he had turned Palkin into an ugly old man he set him in the gorse bushes again.

Mikolai had known what he was about. Now Palkin realized that he was a mere grotesque, he did not want to go to see Kunkel again. If Kunkel's eyes roamed the bushes for him he would duck to hide from her the ruin of his face. Then she would go back into the holly thicket and tears of sap would run down her cheeks.

Despite it all, Palkin did not die. So determined was he to have his revenge that this stopped him from drying up in disappointment. One day, when Mikolai's father came creeping through the undergrowth to find out how well his son performed his task, the poor disfigured stick jumped from its hiding-place and fell at his feet. In half-frightened amazement, the farmer thought that this must be the gift of the Leki, the Spirit of the Woods, for, despite his ugliness, Palkin still bore the stamp of a real work of art. The farmer picked up the walking stick—which was just what the unfortunate Palkin wanted.

When Mikolai's father reached his farm he showed the stick to his wife.

"Look at this magic walking stick which I found in the forest," he said. "It must be the work of the Leki. Why, it looks so alive that if I were to hold it in the draught, I'm sure it would sneeze."

In the fumble of the two pairs of hands, Palkin managed to stick his tip hard in Mikolai's mother's right ear. What a shrill screaming there was!

"Ouch . . . ow . . . oo . . . oo . . . oo . . ! I'll never hear out of that ear again! Husband, that walking stick brings bad luck! Quickly, put it back where you found it!"

The farmer was worried, but he realized that his wife's advice was sensible. And so he made his way back to the clearing. But on his way, he decided instead to go to the castle and give the magic stick to his lord, the Count.

The Nobleman was only too pleased to accept the present. He saw its worth as a work of art. He hurried to show it to the Countess.

"Look, Madame, it is a masterpiece. It must have come from the chisel of a great sculptor. It looks as though it were alive. Why, if I were to bring it too close to the fire, the sweat would pour down its face!"

Palkin repeated his trick once more and struck the Countess in the left eye.

"Ouch...ow...oo...oo...oo..!" she screamed. "I've been blinded! It's an ugly peasants' stick! Quickly, return it to the person who gave it to you!"

The nobleman was just about to send the magic stick back to Mikolai's father, when he changed his mind and sent it to the Governor of the Province.

The Governor was delighted and hurried off to show it to his wife.

"This walking stick is a real curio," he said to her. "Look at the expression on the face. It seems to be alive. If I were to shout *Smirna*! I believe it would jump to attention!"

For the third time Palkin misbehaved. The Governor's wife gave a piercing shriek as he jumped into her mouth.

"Ouch . . . ow . . . oo . . . oo . . . oo . . ! The wicked thing has knocked all my teeth out! Give him back to the person who sent it to you as a gift!"

The Governor was about to return Palkin to the Count, when he suddenly thought of presenting him to the Czar.

The Czar was astonished at so rustic a stick and showed it to the Czarina.

"What workmanship! What stupendous skill! The mouth looks as if it were about to cry: *Long live the Czar*!"

Thereupon, for the fourth time in his life of crime, Palkin smartly struck the Czarina across the nose. She behaved as though a terrorist had made an attempt on her life.

"The murderous villain! He's scarred me for life! Burn him! Hang him!"

The Czar was just about to throw the offending stick out of the window, when in came the Minister of Education. The Czar gave it to him instead.

Having reached the top of the ladder, Palkin now began to slip down again. All went exactly as he wished.

The Minister showed Palkin to his wife—and there was a fine porcelain vase lying shattered on the floor. Enraged at the loss, the Minister handed the unlucky stick to the Governor, who had chanced to visit him about the business of his province.

No sooner had the Governor recognized the stick, than without delay he presented it to the Chancellor of the University. The Chancellor showed it to his wife and there, a huge ink-well, full of black ink in which floated the bodies of countless dead flies, overturned all over her skirt.

In his turn the poor Chancellor got rid of the wretched stick. A schoolmaster had asked him for an interview and it was to him that he presented Palkin. Now this was the very schoolmaster who so expertly boxed the ears of the boys in Mikolai's own village. So here we are again!

The schoolmaster kept the stick—he found it very handy—and so Palkin became the rod of justice in the village school.

Truth to tell, he was as light as a feather on the poor pupils. Just the same they would yell and scream . . . if only to stop the beating!

Soon Mikolai started school, and then it was a very different story. Palkin became as hard as iron once

more and it was about the ears of his old tormentor that he really showed what he was made of. *Slap*! on the left ear: *Smack*! on the right ear. *Slap*! *Smack*! *Slap*! *Smack*! He always whistled down when he was least expected and he always left weals that burned like fire.

This was the revenge for which the poor marred stick had waited so long.

At first Mikolai wept bitter tears of rage. Then he became so unhappy at having his ears so soundly smacked that in his misery he began to feel for the wretchedness of others. Now he understood why Palkin had grown so unkind.

One day, while the schoolmaster lingered over watering the cucumbers in his garden, Mikolai stole the stick and carried it off. He took out his knife and, when he had restored Palkin to his youth and beauty, he planted him next to Kunkel in the clump of holly.

Mikolai went away and forgot all about them, but Palkin and Kunkel took root and grew into a splendid cluster of bushes. Slowly but surely their human faces faded away and they became box-trees once more, leaf by leaf and branch by branch, twining closely together.

They lived together happily for many a year, surrounded by the hum of the bees who swarmed around to sip the honey from their flowers.

# *The Six Candles*

On the wooded slopes of the Mont du Loch lived a man called Master Piero, who made his living as a maker of charcoal. One day as he was tending his fires, suddenly around one of them loomed the shaggy mass of a great big bear. The animal had come to complain

about all the smoke Master Piero was making in the forest. However, the charcoal maker took his remarks the wrong way, for with one stroke of his trusty axe he stretched the bear stone-dead in the bracken.

Master Piero lived off the meat of the bear for the rest of the year, but only off the lean, for he did not like fat. And so with the fat of the late, lamented bear, Master Piero, who was exceedingly pious, made six fat candles. These he planned to light before the Crib in the little church in the valley below on the following Christmas Eve.

When Christmas Eve arrived, Master Piero set off on his long journey to the little church, with the six fat candles in his knapsack. But, alas, the mountainside was thick with snow, and there was not the slightest trace of the path to be found.

Then Master Piero said to himself: "Why don't I go to the woodcutters' camp? They have a special thing that sends the trunks of the trees which they fell, whizzing down on a couple of pulley wheels on a steel wire. *Whirr*, it goes, and before you know what you're down across the valley and over the other side!"

Now Master Piero's luck was in. The camp was empty, for the woodcutters too, had set out on the long walk through the snow for Midnight Mass. What is more, there below the pulley wheels, like a patient horse at the hitching post, hung a massive tree trunk, all ready to set off down the steel wire.

Master Piero clambered astride the timber, dug his heels into its sides and, with a *whirr* the wheels began to turn.

Now the simple mechanism of these pulley wheels would have soon brought my story to a close, had they not, halfway down the wire, begun to screech and then come to an abrupt and grinding stop.

They had jammed fast, and our flying Master Piero flew no more. Instead he hung three hundred feet up above the snowy white side of the mountain, and above *him* was the black of the sky in which hundreds of stars twinkled frostily.

Master Piero soon realized that if he stayed there until daybreak, he would all too likely be turned into frozen meat just as he had turned the bear into smoked meat—with one difference; nobody would want to eat *him*. This, however, was no consolation, but a fresh cause of complaint!

"It's a good thing I've got the candles with me," he thought. "Let's see what we can do with them."

For Master Piero decided that the best thing was to let the woodcutters know his awkward plight so that they would turn back and rescue him.

And so he lit his first little candle.

But alas, wait though he might and call though he did, not a soul appeared. The woodcutters did indeed notice the candle—a point of light twinkling up there behind them—but they mistook it for some under-sized star, the runt of a constellation the moon had littered. The most sensible of the woodcutters thought that there was something odd about it, but then there

is always something odd about the stars on Christmas Eve—and about people, too, and oxen and asses and even about the straw in the stable. And as for Master Piero's cries for help, they were lost in the prayers of the wind, for all Nature prays on Christmas Eve—the winds, the pine trees, key-holes, drains and even the dogs, tied up by their masters so that they do not follow them to church.

The upshot was that the woodcutters continued on their way, and the candle went out, its light being useless.

"What a fool I am to have expected *men* to help me!" Master Piero reflected bitterly. "I should have asked my patron saint!"

So he lit his second candle, set it firmly on the tree trunk beside him and said this prayer: "Dear Saint Peter, good saint of the mountain, come down from heaven and get me out of this!"

Now of course the good Saint Peter would have come instantly to the aid of the poor man, had the prayer reached him, but, alas, on Christmas Eve he had more work than he knew how to do. There were the cribs in all the little churches in the valleys for him to admire, the glow of all the candles to dazzle his eyes and the smell of all the incense to delight his nose. And then he had to listen to all the hymns, and forgive those who sang out of tune; he had to soothe the throats of those with bad coughs and he had to stop the chair legs scraping on the flagstone of the church floors. And so Saint Peter did not hear Master Piero's summons and did not come to his rescue.

Whereupon the second candle, too, flickered out, its light being useless.

When there was no sign of the saint, Master Piero gave up all hope of being rescued from his perch before daybreak, when the woodcutters would return to their camp. Now, as the stars wheeled slowly above his head, his only thoughts were to stay alive until the long night was over and not to tumble into the snow-smothered valley, stretching below him like a shroud.

And so to fight his weariness, the wind and the cold, he ate the third candle—and what a wretched Christmas dinner that was!

And to get some warmth back into his swollen hands he lit the fourth candle.

Then occurred the sort of miracle which rewards the man who stands on his own two feet. By the light of the candle, Master Piero examined the pulley wheel and saw that it was jammed by a rusty section of the steel wire.

"What a fool I've been!" he exclaimed. "I only had to grease it. Why, the wire wanted its Christmas dinner, too!"

This he did with the fifth candle. Then he roused his wooden steed with a couple of kicks from his heels, gave it a jerk to set it going and, *whirr*, he whizzed off and reached his destination safely this time.

He got to the little church just as Midnight Mass was ending, and his sixth candle stood up proudly among the others, now beginning to gutter.

As he lit it before the Crib, Master Piero murmured: "Dear little Lord Jesus the bear is the one who is really offering you this candle. You see, I'm so stupid that if the bear had not been so fat I should have come to you empty-handed!"

# *The Lazy Apple Trees*

Once upon a time there lived near Kyoto—which was what they called Tokyo in those days—a farmer whose name was Hoga. Now he was very cross with his apple trees, for although he had some thirty or more in his orchard, these trees would not produce one single apple. In vain he encouraged them with kindly words, stroking their trunks with the palm of his hand and heaping as much of the richest manure as they liked around their feet. All was of no avail, for they gave him not one single apple in return.

At last he thought of a trick. He whispered it into the ear of his servant, Takuyori, a cheerful, willing lad, and this is what happened.

It was springtime and the orchard was white with blossom when Takuyori climbed into the finest apple tree of all. He was completely hidden by its flowers and, when Hoga took a stroll through his orchard as though nothing in the world were the matter, this is the conversation that passed between them.

"Hear, O Hoga, by the mouth of their eldest brother

what the apple trees in blossom have to tell you! This year they will be barren no more. They swear by Kuku-nochi, the God of the Tree Trunks, and by Hamori, the God of the leaves, that soon they will be covered with as many apples as their boughs can bear."

And Hoga answered: "O beautiful tree, eldest brother of my apple orchard, who thus addresses me, I record the promise which you make in the name of these your brothers. I trust in the word of my brave, true trees. But if this is but a jest to mock me, I swear by Okitsu-hiko, the God of my Kitchen, that I will set my axe to their roots and make them firewood to cook my rice for many a long year."

And then, as though nothing in the world were the matter, he strolled away, and a little later Takuyori came down from his perch.

When they were alone once more the apple trees

took advantage of a gentle breeze to whisper with all their leaves. And this is what they said: "See how we have pledged our solemn word, and all because of that climbing monkey! See how we have been forced into bearing fruit! Let us all seek a means of keeping our oath and at the same time of gaining our revenge!"

And they thought so hard that at last they found a way.

They bore so vast a quantity of fruit that their boughs bent under the weight of it, but every single apple, and there was not one exception, was in the shape of a human head, with two eyes, two ears, a nose and a mouth—just like Takuyori. You could not mistake him, they even wore his cheerful grin and had his wicked twinkle in their eyes.

Hoga thought he would die of laughter when he saw them. Then he had another thought—of all the money he could make from selling these extraordinary apples. So he picked ten baskets full and sent them to the market in Kyoto.

There they were the hit of the day. Hoga had such a crowd of customers that he could only sell them one apple each. And the next day ten more full baskets were sold just as fast. And the day after that, ten more. For a whole month, Hoga did nothing but sell his Takuyori-faced apples one by one, so that his servant's portrait was in every home in the whole Province.

For, as you may imagine, nobody would eat these apples shaped like a human face. They kept them as curios to amuse the children, and placed them on their household altars to rejoice the souls of their ancestors.

And Hoga rubbed his hands at the thought of all the money he had earned.

Now about this time, in his home in the Seventh Heaven, the Great God Kami summoned Yachimata-hiko, the little God of all the Roads and the Bridlepaths and said to him: "I have learned that the Mikado of Japan is preparing to make war to fill his palace with riches. Take him this bag, it is stuffed with the finest and most precious jewels in the whole world, and make him promise to keep the peace."

"But," Yachimata-hiko asked the Great God Kami, "how will I know the Mikado? I have never set eyes on him in my life."

"You will find his portrait in every house in the Empire. So what could be easier?"

The little God of the Roads and the Bridlepaths then set off to earth to perform his task. Before he knew where he was, he was in Kobe. As he made his way to the capital, in every house into which he glanced and at every inn at which he stopped, he saw one of the apples which Hoga had so recently sold. He thought they were all portraits of the Mikado and did not have the least difficulty in remembering exactly what the face looked like.

Thus, no sooner had he reached Kyoto, than he met Takuyori and promptly mistook him for the Mikado. To the servant's astonishment he made him promise never to make war on anybody again (a thing the poor fellow had no difficultly in swearing), handed him in the name of the Great God Kami, the bag of precious jewels, and sped back to Heaven once more.

When Hoga learned of the gift of the gods which had made his servant the richest man in all Japan, he saw in a flash that it was all due to Takuyori's face being on the apples. He therefore resolved, in his turn, to enjoy the fruits of fame.

He hired a new servant and, when Spring came again, made him dress in a suit of his own clothes, while he put on the servant's rags. Hoga then climbed the tallest apple tree, hid himself among the blossom and pretending to address the owner of the orchard, made him the new promise of another bumper crop. The servant replied with an oath to cut down the trees and use them for firewood if they bore no fruit. Believing themselves once more to have pledged their word, the apple trees kept it, again avenging themselves, for lack of anything better, by shaping their fruit into the features of Hoga. As they had done the year before, everyone wanted one of the apples, and the crafty farmer's face was in every house in Honda.

Now, at about this very time, the Great God Kami grew angry with the Mikado, who had carried war into Korea. He summoned Kawa, the little God of the Gurgling Rivers, and this is what he said to him. "I have learned that the Mikado of Japan has broken his word to me and has ravaged Korea. Go, find where he lives and cause a flood to sweep his palace away."

"But," Kawa asked the Great God Kami, "how will I know the Mikado? I have never set eyes on him in my life?"

"You will find his portrait in every house in the Empire. So what could be easier?"

The little God of Gurgling Rivers then set off for earth to perform his task. Before he knew where he was, he was near Gifou and, as he made his way to the capital, in every house into which he glanced and at every inn which he stopped, he saw one of the apples which looked like Hoga. He thought that they were all portraits of the Mikado and did not have the least difficulty in remembering exactly what the face looked like.

Thus, when he reached Kyoto and saw Hoga, he thought he was the Mikado. He followed Hoga to find where he lived and, raising the waters of the stream which flowed through the farm, swept his house away, uprooted his apple trees and covered his orchard with so thick a coat of mud and pebbles that forever after it was a wilderness.